Contents

What a Deal!

Have you ever been excited by a great deal at a store? Perhaps a video game you had really wanted was a lot less expensive than it usually is. Maybe you could buy three games for the price of one. In the early 1800s, the United States got one of the best deals in its history when it bought land in North America.

In 1803, the United States stretched from the Atlantic Ocean in the east to the Mississippi River in the west, and from Canada in the north to Georgia in the south. The land it purchased—the territory of Louisiana—stretched from the Mississippi River in the east to the Rocky Mountains in the west, and from Canada in the north to the Gulf of Mexico in the south. Does this sound like a big piece of land? It should! It measured about 828,000 square miles (2,145,000 sq km) and doubled the size of the United States.

After the Louisiana Purchase, the United States became one of the largest and most **diverse** nations in the world. The Louisiana Purchase inspired many Americans with a spirit of adventure and the desire to settle all the land from the Atlantic Ocean to the Pacific Ocean.

So how did the United States, a new nation with little money, get this land without waging war? To find that answer, let's take a look at the history of the Louisiana Territory.

The Louisiana Territory was much larger than today's state of Louisiana. Thomas Jefferson, the third president of the United States, saw the Louisiana Purchase as an opportunity for the United States to become a more powerful nation.

Thomas Jefferson

Louisiana Purchase

United States at time of Louisiana Purchase

Louisiana, a French Colony

By the seventeenth century, European nations had sent many explorers to claim land in North and South America. In 1682, French explorer René-Robert Cavelier de La Salle traveled down the Mississippi River and claimed a large area of North America for France. He named it Louisiana in honor of France's king Louis XIV.

THE LE MOYNE BROTHERS

In 1699, two French brothers traveled to Louisiana. Pierre Le Moyne d'Iberville and Jean-Baptiste Le Moyne de Bienville believed that Louisiana and the Mississippi River could make France wealthy. Iberville returned to France to ask the French king for money. In 1701, France became involved in a war, and the king felt he couldn't afford to send

René-Robert Cavelier de La Salle

money and men to the North American colony. Iberville died of an illness in 1706. By that time, Bienville had established a good relationship with the Native Americans living in the colony. He began a trading company, but few new settlers arrived.

On this map from the late 1600s, the Louisiana Territory is named La Louisiane, which means "Louis's land." Europeans hadn't explored much of this territory yet.

SLAVERY IN THE NEW COLONY

To raise money for war, in 1712 France sold a **charter** to merchant Antoine Crozat, giving him the sole right to trade in the Louisiana Territory. Crozat began bringing African slaves to the colony. However, he had a difficult time making a profit and gave the trading rights back to the French government in 1717.

NEW ORLEANS IS BORN

By 1718, Bienville was serving as governor of Louisiana. He established the city of New Orleans at the mouth of the Mississippi River, naming it after the ruler of France at that time—Philippe II, Duke of Orléans. In 1721, it became the capital of Louisiana. By 1728, 1,000 colonists lived in New Orleans.

MORE SETTLERS, MORE PROBLEMS

In 1720, the French government gave the colony's charter to a Scottish businessman named John Law. Law had some success attracting new colonists by promising free land. More colonists meant more trade. Settlers continued to bring in

John Law

slaves from the Caribbean islands and Africa. Besides French settlers and slaves, about 2,000 Germans settled north of New Orleans.

However, more colonists also meant more trouble between the French and Native Americans over land and trade. Some Native Americans were even forced into slavery. French soldiers eventually killed nearly all of the Natchez Indians. Fighting between the Chickasaw and the colonists continued into the 1740s.

Mort et Convoi du Serpent piqué

Temple.

This drawing shows the funeral of the Natchez leader Tattooed Serpent. This chief was friendly with the French settlers, but after his death, more conflicts broke out between the Natchez and the French.

The French and Indian War

By the late 1740s, many European countries had claimed land in North America. At times, disagreements regarding the boundaries of these territories led to conflicts. The French and Indian War began over boundary problems in the upper Ohio River valley. Both the French and the British wanted this land, and both already had built trading posts and forts.

In 1749, French forces—**allied** with several Native American tribes—received orders to remove British colonists from the area. By 1754, the British

This picture of the French and Indian War shows British forces, including George Washington (middle), celebrating taking Fort Duquesne (located in what is now Pittsburgh, Pennsylvania) from the French in 1758.

AN AMERICAN HERO

George Washington served with the British during the French and Indian War. Washington was from Virginia, a colony that wanted British control of the Ohio River as a way to expand its trade west. In 1755, at the Battle of the Monongahela, it was said that Washington had two horses shot dead beneath him. Some say he was also hit by four bullets, which got caught in his coat. His courage in battle made him a hero in Virginia. He used his experiences in this war when he fought the British during the American Revolution.

and French were at war, not just in North America, but in Europe and other parts of the world as well. At first, the French had the more powerful army. However, by 1757, France was having great financial difficulties. It didn't have the resources that the British had. By 1763, the French were forced to surrender. On February 10, 1763, they agreed to the Treaty of Paris, giving French territory east of the Mississippi River to Great Britain and French territory west of the Mississippi River, including New Orleans, to Spain.

Changing Hands

By the late 1700s, it was clear that the Louisiana Territory was valuable. The country that owned it had control over the Mississippi River and trade in North America.

SPAIN

After the Treaty of Paris, Spain was slow to send officials to establish Spanish rule over the Louisiana Territory. A Spanish governor finally arrived in 1766, but the French residents were unhappy with his policies. In 1769, a group of 400 people in New Orleans forced the governor onto a ship and ordered him back to Spain. The Spanish king sent soldiers and more governors to take control of New Orleans.

Port of New Orleans

A NEW NATION'S INTERESTS

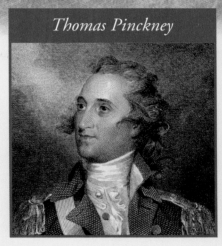

Thomas Pinckney

After the American Revolution had established the United States in 1783, the new nation became interested in the Louisiana Territory for several reasons. Many colonists had settled within its borders. Also, the United States wanted to use the Mississippi River and the port of New Orleans for trade and travel. On orders from President George Washington, the U.S. ambassador to Great Britain,

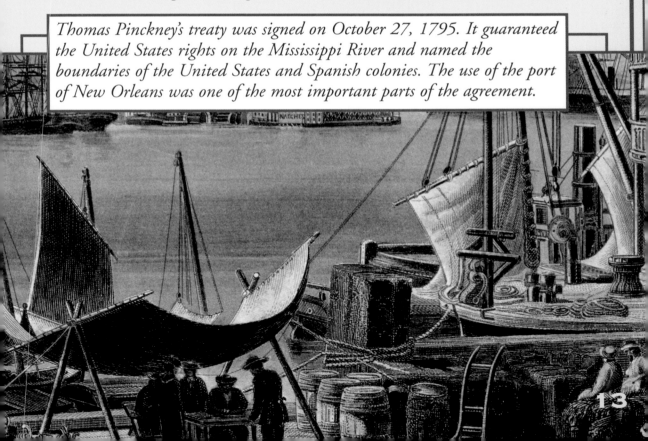

Thomas Pinckney's treaty was signed on October 27, 1795. It guaranteed the United States rights on the Mississippi River and named the boundaries of the United States and Spanish colonies. The use of the port of New Orleans was one of the most important parts of the agreement.

Thomas Pinckney, worked out a treaty with Spain in 1795, allowing Americans to use the river and the port.

A Secret Deal

By 1793, the French government was led by Napoléon Bonaparte. Bonaparte wanted to establish an empire in North and South America. He needed the Louisiana Territory back in French control as a base for this empire. In 1800, Bonaparte secretly forced Spain to give the colony back to France.

At first, the United States only heard rumors of the secret agreement. In 1802, Spanish officials refused to let

Napoléon Bonaparte was a general who helped establish a French empire in the nineteenth century. He was captured by the British in 1815 and imprisoned on an island until his death in 1821.

Americans store goods in New Orleans as they had before. U.S. president Thomas Jefferson wondered what this meant. Did Bonaparte make this order? Would U.S. citizens continue to be able to travel the Mississippi River? Would Bonaparte try to extend the French empire into the United States through war?

Jefferson sent Robert R. Livingston as a representative to Paris, France, with an offer to buy New Orleans. Livingston **negotiated** with Charles-Maurice de Talleyrand for several months. In January 1803, another U.S. official, James Monroe, arrived with orders to pay up to $10 million for New Orleans and the western Florida territories.

Robert R. Livingston

Charles-Maurice de Talleyrand

The Louisiana Purchase

Before Monroe arrived in France, Napoléon Bonaparte had a change of heart. His plans for a North American empire had depended on the sugar crops in the Caribbean islands. His forces had been unable to stop a slave revolt ending French control of the island of Saint Domingue (now Haiti). Bonaparte knew he couldn't build an empire without the wealth of the Caribbean. In fact, Bonaparte needed money to fund a war with Britain to maintain his European **landholdings**. He knew he didn't have a large enough army to protect lands in both Europe and North America. He decided to sell Louisiana.

On April 11, 1803, the minister of the French treasury offered a deal to the U.S. ambassadors. France would sell not just New Orleans but all of the Louisiana Territory for $15 million. Even though Livingston and Monroe only

In this picture, Monroe, Livingston, and Talleyrand discuss the Louisiana Purchase. Livingston later said that the purchase was "the noblest work of our whole lives." It made the United States rank "among the first powers of the world."

had permission to pay $10 million for New Orleans and western Florida, they knew this deal was too good to pass up. This was less than 3 cents an acre (0.4 ha)! By April 30, they had agreed to the purchase.

The treaty was drawn up and sent back to the United States. Exact boundaries had not been stated and would have to be decided later. Jefferson and Congress approved the treaty. The United States took control of Louisiana on December 20, 1803.

CAUSE
After a slave revolt, Napoléon Bonaparte lost control of the French colony of Saint Domingue and the island's valuable sugar crop.

CAUSE
Napoléon Bonaparte was about to fight a war with Britain in Europe but didn't have enough money to fund it.

EFFECT
Napoléon Bonaparte decided to sell Louisiana to the United States to pay for the war.

Arguments in Government

You might be surprised to learn that not all Americans believed the Louisiana Purchase was a good idea. The United States was young in 1803. Many U.S. citizens still disagreed about the powers of the central government and the president.

WORRIES ABOUT THE FUTURE

Many people thought it was a mistake to become friendly with France and feared this deal would start a war with Great Britain. Another worry was that the new land would increase the south's power and the nation would split apart because the north and south had different interests.

LEGAL?

Even Thomas Jefferson believed that the **U.S. Constitution** didn't give the federal government the power to purchase land. However, he was worried Bonaparte would change his mind before the Constitution could be amended. Jefferson hoped future U.S. citizens would believe he "did this for your good."

Most Americans thought the purchase was a good decision. Jefferson's popularity as president increased, and he easily won reelection in 1804.

These people, dressed as French and American soldiers, act out the December 1803 ceremony in which France gave control of Louisiana to the United States.

Jefferson Looks West

Years before the Louisiana Purchase, Thomas Jefferson had believed a route across the continent to the Pacific Ocean would allow the United States to trade with more countries. He also believed that exploring the Pacific Northwest (now Washington and Oregon) before other European nations would help the United States claim this land.

In addition, Jefferson had great interest in the natural resources of the western part of the continent. Legends about this territory said that creatures such as unicorns and beavers taller than people lived there!

On January 18, 1803, Jefferson asked Congress for a small amount of money to fund an **expedition** to explore a northwest route through Louisiana to the Pacific Ocean. He worried that Congress wouldn't allow an expedition across territory that the United States didn't even own yet. He stated that improving the relationship between the United States and the Native Americans in the west could only improve the nation's fur trade. On February 28, 1803, Congress agreed to the expedition.

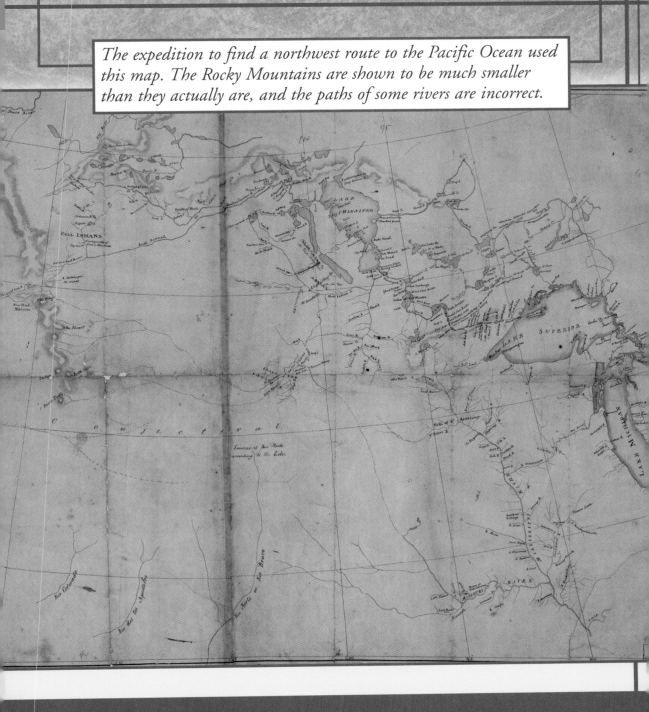

The expedition to find a northwest route to the Pacific Ocean used this map. The Rocky Mountains are shown to be much smaller than they actually are, and the paths of some rivers are incorrect.

The Corps of Discovery

Jefferson chose U.S. Army captain Meriwether Lewis to head the expedition. Lewis asked fellow soldier William Clark to help him lead. Together they gathered over forty-five men—and Lewis's dog—to travel with them. The main purpose of the **Corps** of Discovery was to find a water route to the Pacific Ocean. They also planned to make maps and take notes of their encounters along the way.

William Clark

It Begins

The journey began on July 5, 1803. Meriwether Lewis traveled from Washington, D.C., to western Pennsylvania. Near Pittsburgh, he collected supplies and waited for the expedition's ship to be completed. On October 14, 1803, Lewis and a small crew sailed down the Ohio River and took Clark and some more men on board in Indiana. When the crew reached the Mississippi River, they sailed north. During the winter of 1803 and 1804, they stayed at a camp at the mouth of the Missouri River. By spring, the United States had officially taken possession of the Louisiana Territory.

Meriwether Lewis

Frontispiece

Page 220.

A Canoe striking on a Tree.

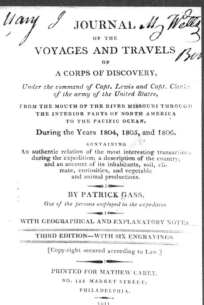

JOURNAL

OF THE

VOYAGES AND TRAVELS

OF

A CORPS OF DISCOVERY,

Under the command of Capt. Lewis and Capt. Clarke
of the army of the United States,

FROM THE MOUTH OF THE RIVER MISSOURI THROUGH
THE INTERIOR PARTS OF NORTH AMERICA
TO THE PACIFIC OCEAN;

During the Years 1804, 1805, and 1806.

CONTAINING

An authentic relation of the most interesting transactions
during the expedition; a description of the country;
and an account of its inhabitants, soil, cli-
mate, curiosities, and vegetable
and animal productions.

BY PATRICK GASS,

One of the persons employed in the expedition.

WITH GEOGRAPHICAL AND EXPLANATORY NOTES.

THIRD EDITION—WITH SIX ENGRAVINGS.

[Copy-right secured according to Law.]

PRINTED FOR MATHEW CAREY,
NO. 122 MARKET STREET,
PHILADELPHIA.
1811.

Journal of the Voyages and Travels of a Corps of Discovery *was written by Patrick Gass—a member of the expedition—in 1811.*

A HELPFUL FRIEND

In May 1804, the Corps of Discovery sailed up the Missouri River. Among the many Native American tribes they met in their travels were the friendly Mandan and Hidatsa tribes of North Dakota. Living with the Hidatsa was Sacagawea (sah-kah-guh-WEE-uh), the Shoshone Indian wife of a French-Canadian fur trader. Sacagawea could speak several languages and could act as an interpreter for the explorers. Lewis and Clark hired Sacagawea and her husband to accompany them on their journey.

SACAGAWEA GOES HOME

Next, the expedition traveled through the Great Plains on the Missouri River. They were forced to take a land route to pass by the Great Falls. They then followed the Jefferson River to the foot of the Rocky Mountains. This was the land of the Shoshone Indians. The Hidatsa had **kidnapped** Sacagawea from the Shoshone when she was young. After speaking with the Shoshone leader, she realized he was her brother! The Shoshone warned the expedition to travel the Rocky Mountains by foot as the water routes were too dangerous.

FINALLY!

On the other side of the Rocky Mountains, the Corps met the Nez Perce Indians. They fed the Corps and helped them make new canoes to sail down the Clearwater and Snake Rivers. Next, the Corps came to the Columbia River. On November 24, 1805, they finally reached the Pacific Ocean.

After spending the winter in a fort they built, the expedition traveled back east, reaching St. Louis, Missouri, on September 23, 1806. Crowds of

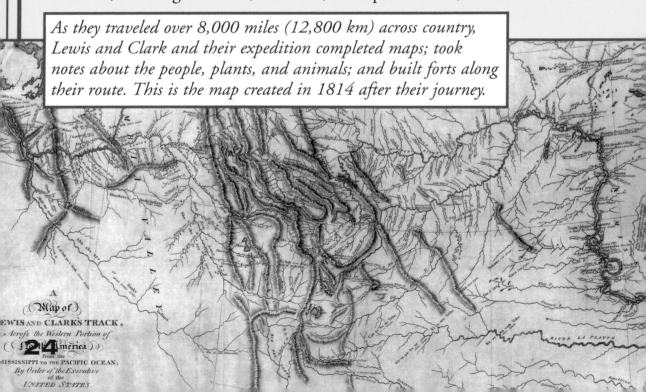

As they traveled over 8,000 miles (12,800 km) across country, Lewis and Clark and their expedition completed maps; took notes about the people, plants, and animals; and built forts along their route. This is the map created in 1814 after their journey.

A
Map of
EWIS AND CLARK'S TRACK,
Across the Western Portion of
America
From the
MISSISSIPPI to the PACIFIC OCEAN;
By Order of the Executive
of the
UNITED STATES.

people greeted them as heroes. Lewis and Clark had not found a water route to the Pacific. However, their 2-year journey through the Louisiana Territory began a period of western expansion.

AN INVALUABLE FRIEND

Do you know which woman has more statues than any other in the United States? Sacagawea! Besides interpreting, Sacagawea was **invaluable** to Lewis and Clark in other ways. She helped guide them to the Rocky Mountains and showed them which plants and roots they could eat. Sacagawea also helped the expedition make friends with other Native Americans who believed the explorers were peaceful because they traveled with a woman. Sacagawea's nickname in the Corps was Janey.

New Land, New Ideas, New Problems

The Louisiana Purchase and the Lewis and Clark expedition helped bring more attention to some national issues. Interest in further western expansion grew among U.S. citizens. Unease about slavery in the new territories also increased.

MANIFEST DESTINY

Manifest Destiny was the name given to the idea that the United States should expand completely across the United States to the Pacific Ocean. The Louisiana Purchase made this idea seem possible. Lewis and Clark's journey strengthened the U.S. claim on the Pacific Northwest as well. More people started moving west than ever before.

THE SLAVERY ISSUE

As more people moved west, new territories and states created from the Louisiana Territory brought up a heated issue—slavery. At this time, most northern states were free states, which meant that slavery wasn't allowed. Southern states allowed slavery as the Louisiana Territory had. For a time, Congress tried to keep a balance of slave and free states. Would the new states created from Louisiana be slave or free states? Eventually, the nation would go to war to decide the slavery issue.

STATES CREATED FROM THE LOUISIANA TERRITORY

the whole state of	part of the state of
Missouri 1821	Louisiana 1812
Arkansas 1836	Mississippi 1817
Iowa 1846	Texas 1845
Kansas 1861	Minnesota 1858
Nebraska 1867	Montana 1889
Oklahoma 1907	North Dakota 1889
	South Dakota 1889
	Wyoming 1890
	New Mexico 1912

This picture shows slaves being sold in New Orleans in 1861.

The New Americans Go to War

The parts of the Louisiana Territory that were settled at the time of the Louisiana Purchase included people of French, Spanish, German, and British **descent**. Thousands of slaves and free blacks from the Caribbean and Africa lived there, too. All of these people spoke different languages, practiced different religions, and were suspicious of their new government. Surprisingly, a war united these people with their new nation.

After British sailors had forced U.S. sailors into their navy and had seized U.S. trading ships, the United States declared war on Britain on June 18, 1812. In December 1814, the British sailed into the Gulf of Mexico and attempted to take the city of New Orleans.

FORCED WEST

At the time of the purchase, Native Americans in the Louisiana Territory included mostly Choctaw in the east and Caddo in the west. At first, some thought they would be given their own nation within the territory. However, the Native Americans were continuously made to move farther west until white settlers completely controlled the Louisiana Territory.

U.S. general Andrew Jackson was charged with stopping the invading forces. Although Louisianans were distrustful at first, they disliked the idea of British rule even more. Jackson put together an army with soldiers of various backgrounds, including blacks, Native Americans, and even pirates! The Americans defeated the British at New Orleans by January 8, 1815.

This scene shows the Battle of New Orleans. Many people in Andrew Jackson's army were promised forgiveness for their crimes if they joined.

A World Power Emerges

The Louisiana Purchase remains one of the great moments in American history. The Louisiana Territory led to new land and new trading opportunities for U.S. citizens. The new size of the United States, along with the military strength shown in the War of 1812, helped it emerge as one of the most powerful countries in the world.

A Timeline of the Louisiana Territory

— 1682   René-Robert Cavelier de La Salle claims Louisiana for France.

— 1699   Pierre Le Moyne d'Iberville and Jean-Baptiste Le Moyne de Bienville explore and set up fur trade.

— 1718   Bienville establishes New Orleans at the mouth of the Mississippi River.

— 1754   French and Indian War begins.

— 1763   Treaty of Paris gives land east of the Mississippi to Great Britain and land west of the Mississippi to Spain.

— 1795   Pinckney's treaty with Spain gives United States use of the Mississippi River and the port at New Orleans.

— 1800   France receives Louisiana Territory from Spain.

— 1803   United States buys Louisiana Territory from France. Corps of Discovery begins exploration of Louisiana Territory.

— 1806   Corps of Discovery returns.

— 1812   Louisiana becomes first state created from Louisiana Territory.

— 1815   Americans defeat British at Battle of New Orleans.

Glossary

ally (uh-LY) To form an association to work together for a common purpose.

charter (CHAHR-tuhr) An official agreement giving someone permission to do something.

corps (KOHR) A group of people with a common purpose acting under common direction.

descent (dih-SEHNT) The line of family from which someone comes.

diverse (dih-VUHRS) Different.

expedition (ehk-spuh-DIH-shun) A trip made by a group of people to explore unknown territory, or the people who go on the trip.

invaluable (in-VAL-yuh-buhl) Having great value that is impossible to calculate.

kidnap (KIHD-nap) To take someone away by force.

landholding (LAND-hohl-ding) An area of land that is owned by someone.

negotiate (nih-GOH-shee-ayt) To talk over and arrange terms for an agreement.

U.S. Constitution (YOO EHS kahn-stuh-TOO-shun) The document adopted in 1788 that explains the different parts of the nation's government and how each part works.

Index

B
Bienville, Jean-Baptiste Le Moyne de, 6, 8, 30
Bonaparte, Napoléon, 14, 15, 16, 17, 18
British, 10, 11, 28, 29, 30

C
Clark, William, 22, 23, 25, 26
Corps of Discovery, 22, 23, 24, 25, 30
Crozat, Antoine, 8

F
France, 6, 8, 11, 14, 15, 16, 18, 30
French, 6, 8, 9, 10, 11, 12, 14, 15, 16, 17, 28
French and Indian War, 10, 11, 30

G
Great Britain, 11, 13, 16, 17, 18, 28, 30

I
Iberville, Pierre Le Moyne de, 6, 30

J
Jackson, Andrew, 29
Jefferson, Thomas, 15, 17, 18, 20, 22

L
La Salle, René-Robert Cavelier de, 6, 30
Law, John, 8
Lewis, Meriwether, 22, 23, 25, 26
Livingston, Robert R., 15, 16
Louis XIV, 6
Louisiana Territory, 4, 8, 12, 13, 14, 16, 22, 25, 26, 27, 28, 30

M
Manifest Destiny, 26
Mississippi River, 4, 6, 8, 11, 12, 13, 15, 22, 30
Monroe, James, 15, 16

N
Native American(s), 6, 9, 10, 20, 23, 25, 28, 29
New Orleans, 8, 9, 11, 12, 13, 15, 16, 17, 28, 29, 30

P
Philippe II, Duke of Orléans, 8
Pinckney, Thomas, 14, 30

R
Rocky Mountains, 4, 23, 24, 25

S
Sacagawea, 23, 24, 25
slave(s), 8, 9, 16, 17, 26, 28
slavery, 9, 26
Spain, 11, 12, 14, 30
Spanish, 12, 14, 28

T
Talleyrand, Charles-Maurice de, 15
Treaty of Paris, 11, 12, 30

W
War of 1812, 30
Washington, George, 11, 13